Spirit
OF A
CHAMPION

R O G E R L I P E

FEB. 9, 2004

COACH GILMORE,
THANKS FOR INVESTING YOUR
LIFE AT S.I.U.
GOD BLESS,

[signature: Roger Lipe]

PROVERBS 31:29

Spirit of a Champion

Roger Lipe

ISBN 1-929478-57-7

Cross Training Publishing
317 West Second Street
Grand Island, NE 68801
(308) 384-5762

This book is manufactured in the United States of America.

Library of Congress Cataloging in Publication Data in Progress.

Spirit
CHAMPION

DEDICATION

This book is dedicated to the people of Sport across Southern Illinois, the USA and throughout the world. Their commitment, passion and love serve to challenge and inspire me daily.

Spirit
OF A
CHAMPION

ACKNOWLEDGMENTS

The author would like to acknowledge the ongoing favor he's received from coaches, athletes and administrative staff at Southern Illinois University at Carbondale. They are a constant source of inspiration and communion for him.

He would also like to acknowledge the years of love and investment by the following people:

Sharon Lipe—wife for over 28 years

Jason and Jen Lipe—son and daughter-in-law

Richard and Anna Lipe - parents

Jim and Betty Glover—father-in-law and mother-in-law

Fred Bishop of No Greater Love Ministries—mentor & friend

Lowrie McCown of 360 Sports—mentor and friend

INTRODUCTION

As I enter my 10th year of ministry in Sport, I realize the great privilege and tremendous responsibility that is mine. Each of these simple devotional thoughts has the student-athletes and coaching staffs of teams at Southern Illinois University as its primary readers. When I read my Bible, I see them in every line of Law, History, Poetry, Teaching and Prophetic writings. I recall the moments of great elation and bitter disappointment from countless days of competition. I can hear the sounds of practice and I smell the aroma of gyms and stadiums. Lately, my Bible is full of similar images from "canchas de futbol" in Honduras, Central America as well as hockey, netball and cricket players from the United Kingdom.

I am amazed at the various avenues afforded me to share these thoughts with others. They are read aloud in pre-game with several teams around the state of Illinois and silently by individuals scattered about the nation. This is the fourth book of such devotions published by Cross Training Publishing. I send a weekly devotion via email to hundreds of people each Monday morning and The Fellowship of Christian Athletes does similarly to thousands through their website daily.

Great privilege and tremendous responsibility are certainly mine. I am humbled by such privilege and am most thankful that our Lord Jesus would entrust it to me. I am challenged by the responsibility and pledge to the reader that I will continue to pursue the goal of helping the people of Sport to fully integrate their lives in Sport with their lives in Christ. May we all passionately express our love for God and our love for each other through Sport and all facets of life.

Spirit
CHAMPION

ISOLATION
Mark 1:12-13

Do you ever feel isolated, cut off, all alone? Though you're surrounded by people, you may still be lonely. Jesus knew that feeling and we can draw some courage and comfort from his experience.

We read about it in Mark's gospel at chapter 1 and verses 12 and 13. "At once the Spirit sent him out into the desert, and he was in the desert forty days, being tempted by Satan. He was with the wild animals and angels attended him."

Now I'm sure none of us has ever been sent out into a desert to be the personal whipping boy for Satan, but I'm sure we've all known some loneliness. Notice who cared for Jesus in his loneliness, the text says that wild animals were with him and angels attended him.

Who is with you on your loneliest days? Probably it's your teammates. Who attends to you when you're at your lowest points? That's probably friends and family. The loneliness comes to everyone, the issue is how we deal with it.

As you prepare for today's competition, lean on your teammates and coaching staff for support in the same way Jesus would have depended on those attending angels. Even in the loneliest moments of this season, look for consolation and companionship from friends and family as an oasis might appear in the desert. Compete strongly today.

TEAMWORK
Ecclesiastes 4:9-10

How critical is good teamwork to your individual success? How much of your success can you directly tie to your teammates and their support? Few of us ever achieve greatly on our own and today's scripture outlines two reasons why.

In the fourth chapter of the book of Ecclesiastes at verses 9 and 10 we read, "Two are better than one, because they have a good return for their work; If one falls down, his friend can help him up. But pity the man who falls and has no one to help him up!"

Number one: Two are better than one because they don't just add to each other, nor do they simply multiply their work, instead two have an exponentially better return for their work. Amazing things can be accomplished by people who align themselves to achieve a goal.

Number two: Even in failure, they're able to recover and to press on toward their goals. If one falls down, the other can help him up, encourage him and the two continue on their way. If we fail while isolated, we're in real danger of being left behind and unable to complete the race.

In preparation for this day's competition, be thankful for your teammates. Be confident in the exponential increase that comes through your unified teamwork. Watch for your stumbling teammate and be ready to help him through the rough spots in the season. Together, we'll achieve more highly than any of us could individually.

SERVANT—LEADERSHIP
Mark 10:42-45

Who is someone from your sport, that if he was to walk in the room right now, we'd all feel compelled to give up our seats, to offer something to drink and to serve in any way possible? Who would be deserving of such respect and admiration?

Jesus was certainly such a person in His day, but He refused such treatment. Why? We can read about His reasoning in Mark chapter 10 and verses 42 through 45, "You know that those who are regarded as rulers of the Gentiles lord it over them, and their high officials exercise authority over them. Not so with you. Instead, whoever wants to become great among you must be your servant, and whoever wants to be first must be slave of all. For even the Son of Man did not come to be served, but to serve, and to give His life as a ransom for many."

With each sentence, Jesus raised the price tag for leadership. He said that greatness comes through service of the team. He said that being first comes as we subject ourselves to everyone else. He now says that to be like Him, means self-sacrifice.

How does that happen in competition? When you put your team's success ahead of your personal achievement, that's self-sacrifice. When you prefer the team's goals to your personal goals, that's great leadership. When you sacrifice your privilege in order to free a teammate to achieve, you're leading like Jesus.

As you approach this day's competition, do so with a predetermined will to lead through service and sacrifice. Pay whatever it costs to free your teammates to achieve at their highest level of the season. Be a team leader like Jesus and give your life as a ransom for many.

11

DEFENSE
Ecclesiastes 4:12

Which seems to be the tougher assignment for you, working a double-team or a simple man-to-man defense? The answer would appear to be obvious, but we often seem to prefer individualism to teamwork.

The writer of Ecclesiastes at chapter 4 and verse 12 writes, "Though one may be overpowered, two can defend themselves. A cord of three strands is not quickly broken."

Though this makes perfect sense to us in theory, many times we bristle at the dynamics that accompany good teamwork. We worry about our teammate not executing his portion of the double-team or we worry about our own performance in it. Thus, we'd rather take our chances alone and rely on our own abilities.

The problem is that the principle is still true, "Though one may be overpowered, two can defend themselves." We're much more powerful when we're working in concert with other competitors, despite the perceived problems.

The second sentence is equally powerful as it mentions a cord of three strands. Not just two, but three. On good teams, the coaching staff is the third strand in every alliance of teamwork and unified competition. The coaches' instruction and strategy completes the cord of power and strength that pulls the team to victory.

In the lives of followers of Christ, the Lord Himself is the third strand in every relationship giving purpose, wisdom and life. He unifies and strengthens

ENEMIES AND ALLIES
Mark 3:6

Do you ever think about the irony that accompanies some of the videotape exchange between your opponents? Some of the bitterest rivals in your conference exchange the best film they have of your team because they both want to beat you. In the world of sport, mortal enemies become momentary allies in order to defeat a common opponent. There was at least one similar instance in the life of Jesus.

In Mark's gospel at chapter 3 and verse 6 we read, "Then the Pharisees went out and began to plot with the Herodians how they might kill Jesus." The Pharisees and Herodians were bitter political enemies, but they found themselves with a common opponent—Jesus of Nazareth.

In your sport, there are times when natural enemies share information in order to beat another team with whom they both must compete. Usually, that team's above them both in the standings. Sometimes their conspiracy of information may even lead them to compromise ethical standards.

What are you to do? Be who you are. Maintain your integrity and compete fairly, even when your opponents cheat and conspire. That's what Jesus did and it's what He would do today.

As you compete today, do so within the rules and to the absolute best of your ability. We'll all be proud if you do and they'll all be sorry.

PATIENCE
Ecclesiastes 7:8

Which is the better part of a baseball game, the first pitch or the bottom of the final inning? Do you prefer to see, a football game's opening kickoff or the "Hail Mary" pass in the last seconds? Does the opening tip of a basketball game or the desperation shot at the buzzer hold more excitement for you? The writer of today's scripture holds the same opinion with one added comment.

In the 7th chapter of Ecclesiastes at verse 8 it says, "The end of a matter is better than its beginning, and patience is better than pride." Just like in sport, the author had found that the end of matters far surpass their beginnings. It's like that in most of life's pursuits. Retirement parties are more fun than the first day on the job. Golden wedding anniversaries are even better than weddings.

In sport, you probably enjoy post-season tournaments more than pre-season conditioning workouts. No doubt. Championship games are lots more fun than the first scrimmages of the season. That leads to the writer's final comment, "...patience is better than pride."

In pre-season, lots of us are full of pride and arrogance. By the end of the season, the ones with patience are obvious to everybody; they're the ones making key plays. The end is better than the beginning and patience is better than arrogant pride.

As you compete today, realize that it's more important who finishes a game than who starts it. Exercise patience and compete wisely, that's much better than being prideful and foolish.

MEASURING PERFORMANCE
Mark 4:24-25

How do you measure an athlete's performance? What is your standard of measure for a player's effort? How do you gauge a competitor's commitment, loyalty or teamwork? Jesus had some sobering comments related to measuring such concepts.

Mark recorded these words of Jesus at chapter 4 and verses 24 and 25, "Consider carefully what you hear.' He continued. 'With the measure you use, it will be measured to you—and even more. Whoever has will be given more; whoever does not have, even what he has will be taken from him."

Jesus seemed to be more concerned with faithfulness than fairness. Fairness would have everyone receive and have the same amount of everything. Jesus rewards those who are faithful with whatever they have. They receive even more, while those who are unfaithful squander even what they have.

We've all seen this in athletes with whom we've competed. The faithful competitor demands the same level of commitment that he gives. He gives the same measure of loyalty that he asks of his teammates. He shows the same kind of teamwork that he expects of his teammates. For the unfaithful, sadly, the principle is still true. They neither give nor receive sufficiently.

As you compete today, you can expect great commitment and teamwork from your teammates, if you have shown the same every day in practice. You can expect great loyalty and effort, if you have given them greatly all through the season. Give your absolute best effort today and watch your teammates reciprocate.

ANGER
Ecclesiastes 7:9

How quickly are you provoked to anger during competition? Would your teammates say that you are slow to anger or that you have a short fuse? Today's scripture explains why it's better to keep a cool head in competition.

In chapter 7 and verse 9 of Ecclesiastes we read, "Do not be quickly provoked in your spirit, for anger resides in the lap of fools."

It's very common in sport for a hot head to suddenly blow up during a competition. They get provoked by some trash talk, by a cheap shot, by a coach's comment or any number of things. They are provoked in their spirits and erupt in a foolish demonstration of anger. Some people even think they compete better when right on the edge of a fit of rage.

There is one very great problem with that. Such anger and rage rest squarely in the lap of fools. One's rage is more often an indicator of foolishness than of greatness in competition. Such anger more often results in technical fouls and penalties than excellence in technique and strategy.

As you compete today, stay under control emotionally. Do not be quickly provoked in your spirit. Rage and anger will only lead to foolish penalties and terrible consequences.

RECRUITING
Mark 1:16-18

During the recruiting process, what would be the most important factors in your decision to attend a university? Would it be something like the beauty of the campus, the prospects for the team or another factor like a perfectly matched field of study? Jesus was an outstanding recruiter and we read today about one of his recruiting calls.

Mark records this exchange between Jesus and some of his soon-to-be disciples at chapter 1 and verses 16 through 18. "As Jesus walked beside the Sea of Galilee, he saw Simon and his brother Andrew casting a net into the lake, for they were fishermen. 'Come follow me,' Jesus said, 'and I will make you fishers of men.' At once they left their nets and followed him."

The remarkable thing about how Jesus recruited was that he appealed to these men squarely within their life calling... they were fishermen and so he spoke to them in fishermen language. He talked to them about fishing. He simply shifted their focus from fish to men.

It's the same for you. Your coaches are shifting your focus from one level of sport and the limited area of competition to a higher level and to greater levels of skill and intensity. It's a big shift and requires a strong focus from each of you.

Will you respond as these men did and follow, 'At once...'? Or will you hedge and hesitate to commit to your team? Let me encourage you to commit fully to your coaching staff, to your team leaders and to each member of your team. As you do, you'll see your whole experience in sport transformed into one that's of the highest order. Compete in such a way today.

UPSETS
Ecclesiastes 9:11

Can you remember a time when you defeated an opponent which was highly favored over you? You might also remember a time when you were picked to win, but somehow the victory slipped away. How does that happen?

The writer of Ecclesiastes saw this in his life and wrote about it in chapter 9 and verse 11. There it reads, "The race is not to the swift or the battle to the strong, nor does food come to the wise or wealth to the brilliant or favor to the learned; but time and chance happen to them all."

We've all been a part of competitions when we knew that the better team did not win. We've all had days when for some reason, we didn't have our "A game" and we lost to an inferior opponent.

What should we make of all this? Simply put, you're never out of a competition, even when terribly overmatched. Conversely, you can never count your opponent out when you seem to be the clearly superior team. Time and chance conspire to keep the lesser team in the contest and to even bring about amazing upsets.

As you prepare for competition, don't dwell on your being the favorite or the underdog. Rather, focus your mind on bringing your absolute best to this game. Do all you can to take time and chance out of the equation.

RESPECT
Mark 6:4

How much respect do you get when you go back to your hometown to visit family and friends? Do they understand who you've become? Jesus knew that we don't automatically get the respect that we're due in our hometowns. It was the same for Him in His day.

We read about it in Mark chapter 6 and verse 4 where it says, "Only in his hometown, among his relatives and in his own house is a prophet without honor." Even for Jesus, the Son of God, this truth of human relations was true.

You can be the player of the year, a hall of fame performer, the MVP on your team and people back home will still remember you as the person you were in grade school. Family will still refer to you as your parents' child. It seems a little disrespectful and it's frustrating to endure.

What should we do when this occurs? Be who you are and don't worry about it. It's just natural for them to think this way. Many times, the folks back home just don't get it. Rather than taking offense, treat it like your little secret. Love them and relate to them in a way they can handle. Sooner or later, they'll wake up to who you are and you'll be afforded the respect you deserve.

As you compete today, do so in a way that is deserving of such respect and give the home folks something to be proud of. Even more than that, compete in a way that deserves God's respect.

GAME PLAN
Habakkuk 2:2

How clearly does your coaching staff outline your game plan? How well do you study and implement each one? Clarity of communication on each end will enable us to compete at the highest level.

The prophet Habakkuk speaks of clear communication in chapter 2 and verse 2, "Write down the revelation and make it plain on tablets so that a herald may run with it."

The Lord told the prophet that his communication should be so plain that it could be written on big signs carried by a man on the run and those who saw him could easily understand the message.

Your season of sport moves like a herald on the run. There is a ton of information coming your way every day. Thus each competition's game plan must be expressed very plainly so everyone may understand it fully and your focus must be clear in order to strongly fulfill it.

As you compete today, concentrate tightly on the game plan. Explain it and execute it to perfection for greatest success.

TRADITIONS
Mark 7:9

Every sport has a set of traditions or practices that are a part of its culture and history. Do any of those things ever violate your conscience or cause you to wonder if you should be involved in them? Jesus had some tough things to say to people in His day about similar things.

Let's listen as He confronts some people about foolish traditions in Mark chapter 7 and verse 9, "You have a fine way of setting aside the commands of God in order to observe your own traditions!" Jesus took these people on as they rationalized their way around the simple commands of God in order to make themselves look good for other people.

If we think everyone else cheats in recruiting, does that make it alright for us to do so? If your sport has a tradition of violently hazing young players, does that make it a good idea? From whom shall we take our cues for ethics within the world of sport? These are all tough questions that we need to consider.

Jesus points straight to the most enduring source of truth in regards to ethical standards. It's the Word of God. The Bible speaks straight to us in relation to all of life, even competition and the ethics we need to compete with fairness and justice.

In today's competition, compete strongly and fairly. Compete with great passion and within the rules of the sport. Compete in a way that honors your teammates, your coaches, your family and even honors God.

DESTINY
Habakkuk 2:3

Have you ever been a part of a team that seemed destined to win? How confident were you as you approached each competition? The prophet Habakkuk wrote about destiny in today's scripture.

At chapter 2 and verse 3 of Habakkuk we read, "For the revelation awaits an appointed time; it speaks of the end and will not prove false; Though it linger, wait for it; it will certainly come and will not delay."

It often seems that our dreams and goals from preseason will go unfulfilled and disappointment will surround our team. Habakkuk would encourage us to not give up so easily.

His attitude is incurably positive and forward looking. He says that success is awaiting our arrival. We should remain confident and hopeful for it will certainly come and will not delay.

That's my encouragement to you today. Live with a sense of destiny. Expect the best to happen rather than the worst. Expect your teammates to make great plays instead of waiting for them to collapse. Even in the worst of times, trust God to bring your marvelous destiny to full fruition.

INTEGRITY
Mark 8:36-37

What would it take for you to compromise your integrity? How much money would it take for your to shave points for gambling interests? What would be the consequences of such actions?

Jesus knew and spoke about such matters in Mark's gospel at chapter 8 and verses 36 through 37, "What good is it for a man to gain the whole world, yet forfeit his soul? Or what can a man give in exchange for his soul?" The obvious answers to these questions are, "No good. Nothing."

No matter the price tag on the item, it cannot equal the value of a clear conscience and a pure soul. Nothing in the world is worth the forfeit of one's integrity.

If you exchange your integrity for any price—you lose!
If you cheat in the classroom to get a grade—you lose!
If you shortcut workouts in practice—you and your team lose!

As you compete today, keep your conscience clean by competing within the rules of your sport. Maintain the purity of your soul through integrity and accountability within your team. Compete thusly and you'll experience great rewards with no pangs of a sullied conscience or a tainted soul.

SKILL
I Chronicles 12:1-2

How would you rate the skills possessed by your teammates and yourself? Are you so skilled that people will be reading about you in 1500 years? Such were the abilities of the mighty men of David.

We read about these mighty men in First Chronicles chapter 12 and verses 1 and 2. There it reads, "These were the men who came to David at Ziklag, while he was banished from the presence of Saul son of Kish (they were among the warriors who helped him in battle; they were armed with bows and were able to shoot arrows or to sling stones right-handed or left-handed; they were kinsmen of Saul from the tribe of Benjamin.)"

These men were ambidextrous with any kind of implement of battle and were very experienced. That's a great team to have if you're on the run from the king.

I'd like to challenge you to work hard in every facet of your sport. Make constant improvements in technique, strength, conditioning, mental preparation and teamwork. Apply yourself fully to every skill and tactic with great diligence.

Compete skillfully in today's contest and maybe we'll be reading about you for a long time.

REFUGE
Psalm 57:1

Where and with whom do you seek refuge when the pressures of competition are getting to you? Do you seek out family, friends, solitude? All those can be good sources of refuge. Where do you suppose is the best?

Psalm 57 and verse 1 reveals a most secure place of refuge. There we read, "Have mercy on me, O God, have mercy on me, for in you my soul takes refuge. I will take refuge in the shadow of your wings until the disaster has passed."

The psalmist sought protection and comfort from God in the middle of a great disaster. He begged for God to be merciful and to hide him.

We might encounter disaster in any number of forms during a season of sport. It could come through injury or illness. It might be a losing streak or a coaching staff transition. The question remains, where will we find refuge when disaster strikes or pressures mount?

May I challenge you to trust God's immeasurable power and protection as a secure place of refuge? He will cover you with his love and compassion until the disaster has passed.

Let God's mercy and love cover you as you compete today. Trust Him to be a rock of refuge from the daily storms of life.

WARRIORS
I Chronicles 12:8

How do you describe your teammates and opponents who compete greatly? You might say things like, "He runs like a …." "She's as strong as an …." "That guy is a …." You may have dropped in words like, gazelle, ox or animal in those blanks. The Bible talks about some warriors so fierce that they looked like lions.

We read about these men in the book of First Chronicles at chapter 12 and verse 8, "Some Gadites defected to David at his stronghold in the desert. They were brave warriors, ready for battle and able to handle the shield and spear. Their faces were the faces of lions, and they were as swift as gazelles in the mountains."

I want those guys on my team! Imagine having teammates whose courage makes them look like lions. How great would it be to have the athletic grace and speed of gazelles to carry into competition? That's how these men are described.

As you prepare to compete today, show the strength of a Clydesdale. Run like a deer. Focus as sharply as an eagle and soar over your opponents. Give your absolute best effort today and leave the description of your performance to the media.

ACHIEVEMENT
Mark 7:36-37

Who is the greatest player you've ever known? Did he do everything well or was there one small flaw in his game? How do you think people perceived Jesus when He was on the earth?

Let's read about how Jesus asked people to act after they had witnessed some of his most amazing deeds of compassion. It's recorded in Mark's book at chapter 7 and verses 36 and 37, "Jesus commanded them not to tell anyone. But the more He did so, the more they kept talking about it. People were overwhelmed with amazement. 'He has done everything well,' they said. 'He even makes the deaf hear and the mute speak.'"

Even when Jesus tried to keep people quiet, they couldn't help but talk about Him. It could be the same with you. When you achieve highly, they'll talk about you too. Even when you play down your accomplishments, they'll still talk.

When that happens, watch your attitude. When they won't quit applauding your achievements, maintain some humility. When your photo is in the paper every day and you're the feature story on the television, remember how fickle the crowd is.

Keep these things in mind as you compete today. If you'll take on Jesus' attitude of humility, you'll not be overly impressed by yourself and you'll be in a perfect position to continue with high levels of achievement and superior performance.

STREAKS
Psalm 90:15

What's the longest losing streak you can remember suffering through? How long does your best winning streak seem in comparison? Why does it seem that losing streaks drag on, but win streaks just whiz by?

Moses knew those dynamics during his lifetime and he wrote about it in Psalm 90 and verse 15. There we read, "Make us glad for as many days as you have afflicted us, for as many years as we have seen trouble."

Moses was just asking for a winning streak to come along to offset the terrible times that they had seen in the recent past. He was not asking to go undefeated, just to get back to the .500 mark.

This encourages me. I am much more comfortable asking God for success as I read this psalm. The Lord knows we grow tired and discouraged when we face a number of losses in a row and He's not offended by prayers like this one He heard from Moses.

As you pray on game day, ask the Lord to reward your work and your persistence. Ask Him to match your losing streaks from the past with similar sized winning streaks in the future. Let's join Moses in his heart-felt prayer to God.

SCOUTING REPORT
Mark 9:30-32

Can you recall a time when your coaching staff told you something about an upcoming opponent that triggered some questions? They're how big? Are they really that good? They're how fast? Why are we playing them? Can we compete with them? Did you dare ask the question or did you bite your tongue, afraid to ask it? Jesus' followers had similar thoughts as they heard some tough information from Him.

We read about this in Mark chapter 9 and verses 30 through 32, "They left that place and passed through Galilee. Jesus did not want anyone to know where they were, because he was teaching his disciples. He said to them, 'The Son of Man is going to be betrayed into the hands of men. They will kill him, and after three days he will rise. But they did not understand what he meant and were afraid to ask him about it."

These men heard some very distressing news from Jesus and were immediately full of questions. They didn't understand what was about to happen, but they were sure it was not good. Why would Jesus even tell them about this? It's like your coaches telling you that your next opponent is unbeatable.

The point of such a discussion is to teach and to prepare. Wise coaches give their teams sobering information about upcoming opponents not to bring them fear, but to lead them to strongly prepare for a great competition.

In today's competition, apply every bit of information you've attained from your coaches, from watching videotape, from each day's practice and let it all lead you to a great victory.

LEADERSHIP
I Chronicles 12:22

Who among your teammates leads in such a way that others will naturally follow along? What difference does that make in your team's performance? In today's scripture we see great leadership in the person of David.

David's leadership is described in First Chronicles chapter 12 and verse 22 this way, "Day after day men came to help David, until he had a great army, like the army of God."

Here's David, a great leader assembling an outstanding team. Day after day people joined him in his pursuits. His team could only be compared with the army of God. That's remarkable leadership.

As you prepare to compete today, be the kind of team that defies comparison. Don't be satisfied with the most natural comparisons to last year's team or the team presently leading the conference. Lead and follow in a way that can only be compared with the army of God.

TEAM LEADERSHIP
Mark 9:35

What are some of the foundational principles of your sport? From whom did you learn them? How many of those principles apply to life beyond your sport? Today, we'll hear from Jesus one great life principle as He talks with his team.

This is recorded in Mark chapter 9 and verse 35, "Sitting down, Jesus called the Twelve and said, 'If anyone wants to be first, he must be the very last, and the servant of all.'" This is totally backward from the way things tend to work in our day. People today who want to be first, rush to the front and manipulate their way into the most prominent position.

Jesus turns the whole world upside down by outlining these principles of team leadership:

He called the Twelve—the most highly committed to Himself. Jesus communicates with these people strongly and directly.

If you desire to be first—take the lowest position with your teammates. Don't push your way to the front or demand privilege. Leadership demands that we serve each other and elevate the others on our team.

It's very simple, I look best in God's eyes when I make others look good in the eyes of everyone else. When I promote and elevate my teammates, we all achieve more highly and we enjoy tremendous team unity. When I elevate myself and promote my own agenda, I diminish my teammates and divide our team.

Search for ways to lead your teammates to victory by serving them and by lifting them up to higher levels of achievement. Speak to them strongly and directly. Elevate your teammates all the way to first place.

RESPECT
II Kings 1:13-14

Have you ever heard a disrespectful comment or seen a gesture by a competitor inflame the competitive edge in his opponent and lead to his/her team's defeat? It happens more often than you can imagine and today's scripture tells about a similar instance.

In the Old Testament book of Second Kings at chapter 1 and verses 13 and 14 it says, "So the king sent a third captain with his fifty men. This third captain went up and fell on his knees before Elijah. 'Man of God,' he begged, 'please have respect for my life and the lives of these fifty men, your servants! See, fire has fallen from heaven and consumed the first two captains and all their men. But now have respect for my life!"

This man was much wiser than the two who preceded him. They showed terrible disrespect for the Man of God and were consumed with fire. He knew that Elijah was not someone to be messed with and he took an appropriate posture.

As we compete, we might be better off letting sleeping dogs lie. If your opponent is struggling and seems to be a little off his game, don't trash talk him into a better performance. Rather than showing him up with your mouth, give him proper respect and maybe he won't destroy you in the second half.

WORLDLY LEADERSHIP
Mark 10:42-43

From whom did you learn your leadership style? Do you tend to emulate a coach or team leader from past teams? Who might we find to be examples of poor leadership? Jesus points to some of each in today's scripture.

At Mark chapter 10 and verses 42 through 43, we read, "You know that those who are regarded as rulers of the Gentiles lord it over them, and their high officials exercise authority over them. Not so with you. Instead, whoever wants to become great among you must be your servant..."

There are plenty of models for poor leadership and Jesus pointed directly at one in this passage. He said, "Don't do it like them!" He then laid out simple, direct ways to lead in a way that most honors God and best honors your teammates.

The world's supposed leaders pull rank all the time—don't do that! Their poor leaders lead purely by position and power—you don't have to! Not so with you—don't give in to that lowest and most crude level of leadership! If you want to be great—be a servant to your teammates!

That ethic certainly seems upside down to us, but it is full of wisdom. Jesus knows that the greatest leaders don't need to push their way around with position and power, but they lead by seeking the best for their teammates.

As you compete today, be team leaders like Jesus and seek the best for your team and for individual teammates. As you do, you'll find yourself becoming a great leader and you'll find your team being greatly successful.

COMMITMENT
I Kings 19:19&21

Who is the greatest example of total commitment in your sport? Who has really committed him/herself 100% to your team and to excellence in competition? How would you rate your level of commitment? In today's scripture we see a striking picture of radical commitment.

In the first book of Kings at chapter 19 and in verses 19 and 21 we read, "So Elijah went from there and found Elisha son of Shapat. He was plowing with 12 yoke of oxen and he himself was driving the twelfth pair. Elijah went up to him and threw his cloak around him.... So Elisha left him and went back. He took his yoke of oxen and slaughtered them. He burned the plowing equipment to cook the meat and gave it to the people, and they ate. Then he set out to follow Elijah and to be his attendant."

Elisha was a wealthy farmer plowing his ground until Elijah the prophet came to town. By throwing his cloak around him, Elijah was inviting Elisha to join him in his work. Sounds a lot like a recruiting visit. At that point things changed radically for Elisha. He committed everything to the pursuit God's will.

Elisha slaughtered his oxen and cooked them over a fire made from the plow. That's like a modern farmer blowing up his tractors. The end result is the same; neither is going back to farming. That is what total commitment looks like.

My challenge to you today is to similarly commit to an absolute, whole-hearted, 100% effort in this competition. Cast caution to the wind and hold nothing in reserve. Be as desperate and radical as Elisha in your commitment to your team.

THE GREATEST
Mark 10:42-44

Which of these would most people see as being greater, the driver of the team bus or the star player riding in the back? Which would appear to be more important, the star athlete or the trainer who hands her a bottle of water? Who would seem greater, the guest of honor at the team banquet or the person washing the dishes? We know what most would say, but what do you think? What would Jesus say?

We can read about Jesus' value system in the book of Mark at chapter 10 and verses 42 through 44, "You know that those who are regarded as rulers of the Gentiles lord it over them, and their high officials exercise authority over them. Not so with you. Instead, whoever wants to become great among you must be your servant, and whoever wants to be first must be slave of all."

While totally turning the value system of the world upside down, Jesus said that the great ones are those who serve and that the ones who want to be first must be slaves to the others. Ouch! That doesn't feel good at all.

The problem is that He's right. The bus driver is actually more important to the trip than the one riding in the back.

Greatness comes through service of your teammates. Being first comes at an even higher price—self-sacrifice.

As you compete today, keep in mind that being great will come as you serve your team and that being first is a direct result of putting everyone's needs ahead of your own.

RENEWED STRENGTH
Isaiah 40:28-29

Where do you find strength for competition when you've become weary? Who is your source of power when your legs, arms, back and even your mind is tired? Today's scripture suggests an ideal source.

In Isaiah's book of prophecy at chapter 40 and verses 28 and 29 we read, "Do you not know? Have you not heard? The Lord is the everlasting God, the Creator of the ends of the earth. He will not grow tired or weary, and His understanding no one can fathom. He gives strength to the weary and increases the power of the weak."

Isaiah is confident of the power and strength of God. He knows Him as the Creator of the whole universe, possessed of limitless ability and infinite might. That builds his confidence as he knows God to be gracious and giving of those same attributes.

Everyone who competes becomes weary and feels a loss of power and strength. That is the perfect time to trust God and to commit more than ever to your relationship with Him. He freely gives strength and power. He delights to do so as we simply ask for it and trust Him to supply all that we need.

In your preparation for competition today, ask God for a transfusion of His power in your body. Petition Him for a gift of strength and wisdom for your mind. Pray for and seek more of His love and mercy in your spirit. He'll answer you from His limitless supply, right on time.

OVERCOMING UNBELIEF
Mark 9:23-24

What do you have trouble believing when you consider your team's prospects for the season? Can you believe you'll be conference champions? Can you believe you'll have a winning season? Do you believe you'll defeat your strongest rival? Do you really believe you'll win today's contest? Jesus saw a strong link between what we believe and what we achieve.

His words on this are recorded at Mark chapter 9 and verses 23 through 24, "If you can?' said Jesus. 'Everything is possible for him who believes.' Immediately the boy's father exclaimed, 'I do believe; help me overcome my unbelief!'"

The father of a terribly tormented child came to Jesus for help, asking if Jesus could do anything. Jesus strongly challenged the father that it was not a matter of ability, but a matter of belief. The man responded well to Jesus' challenge and asked for help in overcoming his unbelief.

The same is true for this team and each of you today. You have plenty of ability to compete at the highest level. The question for us is, "Do we believe it?" What can we do to overcome our unbelief?

Unbelief is overcome through committed relationships. As you commit strongly to your teammates and coaches, your trust and belief in their abilities is strengthened. As you commit to struggling teammates, their own belief in their abilities becomes stronger and more powerful. As you grow the trust and accountability on your team, everyone's unbelief is overcome and you can do anything. In today's competition, believe and achieve!

HOPE
Isaiah 40:30-31

Which is more draining to your heart for competition, physical fatigue or a sense of hopelessness and despair? Many times, these two thieves arrive at the same time.

Isaiah writes about the solution to both fatigue and despair in chapter 40 and verses 30 and 31. There we read, "Even youths grow tired and weary, and young men stumble and fall; but those who hope in the Lord will renew their strength."

In every season, each of us will certainly encounter a time when we're absolutely worn out. Our minds and bodies are just drained of strength and even our spirits are devoid of enthusiasm. These are the toughest moments in sport, because the season will continue with or without us.

This scripture breathes hope into our deflated chests as it points directly to the Lord as the one who renews the body, the soul and the spirit. This happens as we trust God with our lives. It comes to us as we place our hope in His love for us. We're energized as He renews our strength through daily communion with Him.

As you compete today and you find your legs weary, trust God for a renewal of strength. Breathe a silent prayer for help when it seems your team is stumbling. Ask the Lord to meet you at every moment of the competition and you'll experience His presence and strength.

TESTS
Mark 10:21-22

What are the most difficult tests for you as an athlete? Do you find the athletic testing hard? How about academic tests? How well do you measure up when your character is tested?

In Mark chapter 10 and verses 21 and 22, we watch as Jesus gives a man a test in character. "Jesus looked at him and loved him. 'One thing you lack,' he said. 'Go, sell everything you have and give it to the poor, and you will have treasure in heaven. Then come, follow me.' At this the man's face fell. He went away sad, because he had great wealth."

This man failed Jesus' simple test in character. I wonder how well we'd do if given a similar test.

If asked to forfeit our position on the team, would we comply? If asked to give up our prospects of success for the future, would we risk it? If asked to even walk away from playing this sport, would we do it? How badly do we want to achieve our goals?

I'd like to challenge you to pay whatever it costs to pursue your goals. Compete without regard to the personal cost as you seek the best for your team. Give all you have in order to help your team be victorious today. As you do, you'll pass the character test with flying colors.

SOAR
Isaiah 40:30-31

What part of your sport comes so easily to you that you seem to effortlessly soar in it? When does competition seem to flow naturally and relaxed? The prophet Isaiah knew of such feelings and writes about them in today's scripture.

At Isaiah chapter 40 and in verses 30 and 31 it says, "Even youths grow tired and weary, and young men stumble and fall; but those who hope in the Lord will renew their strength. They will soar on wings like eagles; they will run and not grow weary, they will walk and not be faint."

What an exciting promise! As we trust God, as we place our hope in His love for us, we will be renewed and able to soar like eagles. Can you really believe that simply trusting Christ will make a real difference in your performance on the field of competition? What do you have to lose?

As you prepare to compete today, take the chance to ask God for His transforming power in your weary, aching body. Ask Him to strengthen your tired legs and to breathe courage into your fainting spirit. Trust strongly and compete courageously.

DISTRACTIONS
Mark 11:7-8

Can you recall the feelings of arriving home after winning a championship or a victory over your fiercest rival? How did you keep your mind focused on your sport and not get distracted by all the noise?

In Mark chapter 11 and verses 7 and 8 we can see how Jesus handled similar circumstances in his life. There we read, "When they brought the colt to Jesus and threw their cloaks over it, he sat on it. Many people spread their cloaks on the road, while others spread branches they had cut in the fields. Those who went ahead and those who followed shouted, 'Hosanna! Blessed is he who comes in the name of the Lord! Blessed is the coming kingdom of our father David! Hosanna in the highest!' Jesus entered Jerusalem and went to the temple."

When I read this I see a team bus coming back into town having just won a championship and crowds of fans waiting for the team on the edge of town. Everyone is excited, honking horns, screaming and shouting congratulations to the team. Imagine how Jesus and His followers must have felt.

Watch Jesus' reaction and gain some wisdom about how to handle success. Does He get caught up in all the excitement and lose His head in the adulation? No, rather He maintained His focus on His mission. He went straight to work on accomplishing His purposes at the temple.

Let's learn from Jesus and keep our minds focused on our team goals even when we're surrounded by people telling us how great we are. Let's not be distracted by the adulation of fans or the fawning of sports reporters.

RESOLVE
Isaiah 50:7

Have you ever known a competitor who seems to have an unbending will to win? One he set his mind on his goal, he would not waiver from it for anything. Perhaps you're like that. Many of the greatest competitors are.

In Isaiah's book of prophecy at chapter 50 and verse 5 we read about such an attitude of resolve, "Because the Sovereign Lord helps me, I will not be disgraced. Therefore have I set my face like a flint, and I know I will not be put to shame."

Some of us are so committed to our goals that, on game day, our faces look like they're carved out of stone. Our resolve is so strong that we're unfazed by outside noises or distractions.

Though he was exposed to possible disgrace and shame, Isaiah pressed on in the pursuit of his goals. He did so because he had a profound trust in God and sensed His help day to day.

As you compete today and as you press toward the completion of this season, set your face like a flint. Focus strongly on your team's goals and let nothing deter you from their fulfillment. Trust in your teammates, your coaching staff and ultimately in your God to help you in this marvelous pursuit.

Spirit
CHAMPION

REPRESENTATION
Mark 12:17

How much of your personal success do you owe to your team? How many hours per week are reasonable for you to practice? Who determines the proper amount of preparation that is necessary for each competition? To whom are you responsible for the most important parts of your life?

Jesus spoke about such matters at Mark chapter 12 and verse 17, where it says, "Give to Caesar what is Caesar's and to God what is God's.' And they were amazed at him."

Let's think about this in athletic terms. If you're wearing the uniform of your school—you must give your allegiance to the leadership they've appointed for your team. If you've accepted a scholarship from a university—you must submit to your coaching staff. While you're on your own time, away from team responsibilities—you must make your own choices about behavior. When you're on your own—give God first priority as you direct your life.

As you compete today, be mindful that you represent a number of people beyond yourself. You certainly represent your teammates, your school, your family and friends, and many of you represent your God. Compete in such a way that they can each be proud of you and that displays your allegiance to each with pride.

JOY AND PEACE
Isaiah 55:12

Which of these is a better descriptor of your frame of mind in competition; joy and peace or anxiety and rage? I've known competitors from both camps and I know which ones were more successful and were better teammates.

Isaiah wrote these words in chapter 55 and verse 12, "You will go out in joy and be led forth in peace; the mountains and hills will burst into song before you, and all the trees of the field will clap their hands."

Though many competitors pursue their sport in anger, full of anxiety and rage; this scripture presents another alternative. If we go out in joy and are led in peace, we find the whole course of life more pleasant and we receive great favor with those around us.

Joy is simply emotional stability. That's most important during competition as we experience the inevitable swings of momentum from one team to the other. If we go out in joy, we have the emotional stability to react appropriately to each situation that arises.

Peace is the capacity to be calm in the midst of chaos and confusion. Competition is full of moments of confusion and we're too often overcome by it. Peace gives you the ability to keep your mind focused on your assignment even when everything seems to be coming unglued.

Pray for the capacity to remain calm and under control, even in chaotic situations. Seek God's character of joy to keep your emotionally afloat in the midst of a turbulent sea of momentum shifts. Compete with a joyful, peaceful heart today.

SOLITUDE
Mark 1:35-37

What do you do to quiet your mind and to keep some perspective about your life? Where do you go to relax, reflect and to meditate? How do you stay true to who you are when everybody is praising you? We'll read today about how Jesus did all of these.

Mark writes about Jesus' life of solitude and focus at chapter 1 and verses 35 through 37, "Very early in the morning, while it was still dark, Jesus got up, left the house and went off to a solitary place, where he prayed. Simon and his companions went to look for him, and when they found him, they exclaimed, 'Everyone is looking for you.'"

Jesus had a unique quality in his life that most of us miss. He valued solitude over popularity. He maintained clarity of thought about who He was, about His values and about His life goals while in quiet reflection, free from the flattering crowds. He knew that it's very easy to pander to a crowd of people who tell you that you're great. He was more concerned with pleasing His Father in Heaven.

We can each carry a similar commitment related to our team. Let's be more committed and responsive to our teammates and coaching staff than we are to the fickle opinions of fans and sportswriters. Let's remember to value those who know us privately and their commitments to us. Let's value them more than those who only know us from what they see on game day and in public. Compete powerfully today and honor those who are most committed to you.

PRAYER
Isaiah 59:1

What do you pray about your life in sport? Do you regularly talk with God about each situation or just when things seem out of control? Which kind of prayer do you think God hears well? My answer may surprise you.

Isaiah the prophet wrote about prayer at chapter 59 and verse 1, there we read, "Surely the arm of the Lord is not too short to save, nor His ear too dull to hear."

It's exciting to me to know that God doesn't discriminate between my weakest prayers of panic and my most serene prayers of thanksgiving. He clearly hears both kinds. What's more, He is responsive to both with His strong arm of protection and deliverance.

In today's competition, invite the Lord into each moment of the game. Pray during pre-game, asking for His help and protection. Pray as the competition reaches its height, seeking His power and wisdom for excellence. Pray after it's all over, give thanks for the privilege of competing and for the win or the loss.

God's more than willing to hear from you on your best day or at your worst moment.

OPPORTUNITY
Mark 14:3-7

Can you recall a time in your sport career when things were so good that you didn't want them to end? You wanted that winning feeling to last for days, but it was soon gone. Jesus had similar days and we can read about some of them.

In Mark chapter 14 and verses 3 through 7 we read, "…A woman came with an alabaster jar of very expensive perfume, made of pure nard. She broke the jar and poured the perfume on (Jesus') head. Some of those present were saying indignantly to one another, 'Why this waste of perfume? It could have been sold for more than a year's wages and the money given to the poor.' And they rebuked her harshly. 'Leave her alone,' said Jesus. 'Why are you bothering her? She has done a beautiful thing to me. The poor you will always have with you, and you can help them any time you want. But you will not always have me."

Focus on the words, "The poor you will always have with you, but you will not always have me," and remember the greatest moments of your athletic career. Think of how precious those feelings and memories are to you. Now when you recognize a similar moment, adopt Jesus' philosophy and drain every drop of good from it.

When another great victory arrives, stay there as long as you can. Savor the moment and grasp its significance. The necessary, mundane things of life are always there, but moments like these are fleeting and few. Recognize them and enjoy them to the fullest. Compete well today and you may just create such a moment.

APPEARANCE VS. HEART
I Samuel 16:7

How do you judge your teammates' performance on game day, by their appearance during pre-game or by their play during the competition? I wish the answer was as obvious to everyone as it is to you and to God. In fact the Bible shares a story of the vast difference between outward appearances and matters of the heart.

In the First Book of Samuel at chapter 16 and verse 7 we read, "But the Lord said to Samuel, 'Do not consider his appearance or his height, for I have rejected him. The Lord does not look at the things man looks at. Man looks at the outward appearance, but the Lord looks at the heart."

Samuel had come to a man's house knowing that the next king of Israel would be there. He was all set to look for the tallest, strongest and brightest of the sons. The Lord stopped him short in his search and clarified His values. Samuel was to see beyond the outward and to look for the heart of a leader.

People are often fascinated by the flashy player who puts on a great show in pre-game, only to wonder why that one never sees any playing time. They're looking at the outward appearance and can't see what the coach sees every day in practice.

As we compete today, let's not fall into the trap of judging by outward appearances. Rather, let's look into the hearts of our teammates and coaches. Let's see clearly and make wise decisions regarding this game and all of life.

ABANDONED
Mark 15:33-34

Have you ever felt abandoned by your team during competition? You look around and wonder, "Where did everybody go? I feel like I'm out here all alone!" Imagine how Jesus felt on a very dark day in His life.

This darkest of days is recorded in Mark chapter 15 and verses 33 through 34, "At the sixth hour darkness came over the whole land until the ninth hour. And at the ninth hour Jesus cried out in a loud voice... 'My God, my God, why have you forsaken me?'"

This was the biggest, most important day of Jesus' life. This was the culmination of His life's purpose. In such a moment, He'd been abandoned by His followers, was even betrayed by one. Worst of all, He felt abandoned by God. In spite of how He felt, He fully completed His mission and honored God to His last breath.

Competition at the highest levels is not always pleasant. It is surely not always fun. You'll occasionally feel like you're all alone in the fight. Don't give in to discouragement and the temptation to quit. You could be on the threshold of a breakthrough for yourself and for your team.

Compete strongly today. Press through your feelings and honor God with your life as a competitor.

UNDERDOGS
I Samuel 17:48-50

What's the greatest mismatch in competition that you've ever experienced? On which side of the mismatch were you? Were you the underdog or the heavy favorite? What was the outcome?

We read about such a conflict in First Samuel chapter 17 and verses 48 through 50, "As the Philistine (Goliath) moved closer to attack him, David ran quickly toward the battle line to meet him. Reaching into his bag and taking out a stone, he slung it and struck the Philistine on the forehead. The stone sank into his forehead, and he fell facedown on the ground. So David triumphed over the Philistine with a sling and a stone; without a sword in his hand he struck down the Philistine and killed him."

Here in one of history's greatest mismatches—the underdog, the little guy, David—kills the overwhelming favorite—the giant, Goliath with a sling and a rock. Notice David's attitude in competition, he ran quickly toward the battle line to meet the giant. No fear, no hesitation, no intimidation. He was ready and willing to give his all.

As you compete today, cast off any fear or intimidation that you may feel of today's opponent. Compete with confidence, sling your stone, slay the giant then cut off his big, ugly head.

Spirit
CHAMPION

COMMITMENT
Mark 1:19-20

What have you left behind to pursue your athletic career? Many of you left your families hours away. Many more left your best friends and possibly even a relationship with a potential spouse. What do you suppose that Jesus' disciples left when he asked them to follow him? We get to see the price of such decisions in the writings of Mark.

At chapter 1 and verses 19 and 20, Mark writes, "When he had gone a little farther, he saw James son of Zebedee and his brother John in a boat, preparing their nets. Without delay he called them, and they left their father Zebedee in the boat with the hired men and followed him."

These men walked away from their family business and their whole careers as fishermen to follow this man Jesus. That's what total commitment looks like.

You've shown similar commitment and you are to be commended for it. You walked away from your family, friends, everything that was familiar and comfortable to you to come to a strange place and strange people.

We must now show the same kind of commitment to our team and to the coaching staff that we've always shown to our family and friends. Demonstrate family-like commitment and loyalty to your teammates as you compete strongly together today.

COURAGE
Joshua 1:6-7

When does your sport demand courage of you? Is it when you face superior competition? Does playing through injuries require courage? Is courage a factor in overcoming fatigue? What role does courage play in overcoming adversity? Today's scripture links strength and courage in a powerful combination.

In the historical book of Joshua in the first chapter and verses 6 through 7 we read, "Be strong and courageous, because you will lead these people to inherit the land I swore to their forefathers to give them. Be strong and very courageous. Be careful to obey all the law my servant Moses gave you; do not turn from it to the right or the left, that you may be successful wherever you go."

Joshua had just taken leadership of his people after Moses had died and this was what God told him as he assumed this most intimidating role. Twice God said to be strong and courageous. The second time He said to be very courageous. Courage would obviously be a most important quality for Joshua's leadership.

What are the situations in today's competition that may require you to be strong and very courageous? You probably thought of some as we opened the issue earlier. Some of those could be as scary to you as replacing Moses would have been to Joshua.

The Lord's word to you today is the same as it was to Joshua, several millennia ago. He would say, "Be strong and very courageous." Walk boldly into today's competition with strength and confidence.

SECURITY
Psalm 37:23-24

How secure do you feel in your game? Is your position on the team rock-solid and secure or a little tenuous? From where does your security for life in sport and life in general come?

King David shares with us the source of his security in the words of Psalm 37 and verses 23 and 24. There we read, "If the Lord delights in a man's way, he makes his steps firm; though he stumble, he will not fall, for the Lord upholds him with his hand."

This man was far from perfect; in fact he had some terrible character flaws. However, he maintained his relationship with God as first priority. Because of that he was very secure.

Some of us find our security in our strength, speed, skills or technical abilities. The problem is that none of those will endure for ever. They will all dissipate over time.

The key to real security over time is relationship. As we maintain our relationships with teammates, we find greater security on our team. As we commit strongly to friends and family, we're ever more secure off the field of competition. As we build a deep, loving relationship with Christ Jesus, all of life is upheld by the secure, strong hands of God.

INTIMIDATION
Joshua 5:1

What advantages are yours when you know your opponents are intimidated by you and your teammates? Do you ever sense their fear? Can you see them hesitate or compete tentatively? Have you watched as the intimidated team was overcome by a momentum shift? Such intimidation is not limited to the arena of sport. In today's scripture, we see it in the Bible.

In the Old Testament book of Joshua at chapter 5 and verse 1 it says, "Now when all the Amorite kings west of the Jordan and all the Canaanite kings along the coast heard how the Lord had dried up the Jordan before the Israelites until we had crossed over, their hearts melted and they no longer had the courage to face the Israelites."

Did you hear how Joshua described the intimidation felt by his opponents? He said their hearts melted and they no longer had the courage to face them. This happened because of the stories being told by others.

This happens all the time in sport. Teams read the newspaper or watch the polls on the web and hear stories of how powerful their upcoming opponents will be. Often, just hearing the news is enough to melt their hearts and to drain every drop of courage from their souls.

As you approach today's competition, expect the news about your team to have made it to your opponent's locker room. Watch for the ferocity of your competitive drive to melt their hearts. Look for the opportunity to drive the courage from the souls of your opponents and to achieve a great victory.

COMMITMENT
Psalm 37:5-6

To whom and to what are you most committed? What do you expect to come from those committed relationships? Today's scripture tells of a person who is worthy of such commitment and one who rewards commitment greatly.

In Psalm 37 at verses 5 and 6 we read, "Commit your way to the Lord; trust in him and he will do this: He will make your righteousness shine like the dawn, the justice of your cause like the noonday sun."

As we commit ourselves to God and trust him with the details of life, he's very faithful to reward us and to even make us look good. This text says that our righteousness will shine like the dawn. Just like the rising son, the issues of life become more plain and we know exactly what to do. It says that the justice of our cause will shine like noonday. Even those around us will see the shining result of our commitment and trust as we justly pursue God's will.

In today's competition, commit everything about yourself to God's wise care. He's fully trustworthy with every part of life, even sport. Entrust your whole life to him and watch as he strongly supports you in every way.

POWERFUL TEAMMATE
Joshua 5:13-14

Have you ever had a teammate of whom you'd say, "I'm glad he/she's on our team? I really don't want to be his/her opponent." There is a story in the Bible of just such a person.

In Joshua's book of history at chapter 5 and verses 13 and 14 it reads, "Now when Joshua was near Jericho, he looked up and saw a man standing in front of him with a drawn sword in his hand. Joshua went up to him and asked, 'Are you for us or for our enemies?' 'Neither,' he said, 'but as commander of the army of the Lord I have come.' Then Joshua fell facedown to the ground in reverence, and asked him, 'What message does my Lord have for his servant?"

Joshua didn't really understand to whom he was talking as he encountered this man. It didn't take long, however, for him to get a clear picture of who was the greater person.

It may be the same with you and your teammates. After just a few practice sessions you probably knew who the superior athletes were. Your probably saw right away who the leaders were. With such people, it's not a matter of them being for or against us; it's more a matter of being sure we're on their side.

In today's competition, be sure to closely align yourself with your teammates and coaching staff. They're for you. Be thankful them and the privilege you have of being on their team. I'm praying that we're all with the commander of the Lord's army. He's the ultimate victor.

ABANDONED
Mark 15:33-34

Have you ever felt abandoned by your team during competition? You look around and wonder, "Where did everybody go? I feel like I'm out here all alone!" Imagine how Jesus felt on a very dark day in His life.

This darkest of days is recorded in Mark chapter 15 and verses 33 through 34, "At the sixth hour darkness came over the whole land until the ninth hour. And at the ninth hour Jesus cried out in a loud voice... 'My God, my God, why have you forsaken me?'"

This was the biggest, most important day of Jesus' life. This was the culmination of His life's purpose. In such a moment, He'd been abandoned by His followers, was even betrayed by one. Worst of all, He felt abandoned by God. In spite of how He felt, He fully completed His mission and honored God to His last breath.

Competition at the highest levels is not always pleasant. It is surely not always fun. You'll occasionally feel like you're all alone in the fight. Don't give in to discouragement and the temptation to quit. You could be on the threshold of a breakthrough for yourself and for your team.

Compete strongly today. Press through your feelings and honor God with your life as a competitor.

EMERGING LEADERS
Judges 11:4-7

How do leaders emerge from among your teammates? Is there a personality type or a position on the team that automatically makes one a leader? Be careful, sometimes the best leaders appear from the most unlikely places. One such leader is seen in today's scripture.

In the book of Judges at chapter 11 and verses 4 through 7 we read, "Some time later, when the Ammonites made war on Israel, the elders of Gilead went to get Jephthah from the land of Tob. 'Come,' they said, 'be our commander, so we can fight the Ammonites.' Jephthah said to them, 'Didn't you hate me and drive me from my father's house? Why do you come to me now, when you're in trouble?'"

Jephthah was an illegitimately born child who nobody cared for, but he grew up to be a mighty warrior. Suddenly, when the people were in trouble, they came to him to be their leader. There must have been something special about Jephthah for the people to reach beyond their prejudice to seek his leadership.

It could be the same among you. Watch and listen to your teammates. Look for and encourage the leaders who emerge, even if they don't fit into your previous leadership profile. These leaders are often God's gift to a team.

As you compete today, respect and loyally follow your team leadership. Your coaching staff and the leaders among your teammates may lead you out of real trouble and into tremendous victory.

MISUNDERSTOOD
Mark 3:20-21

Are you sometimes misunderstood by your family and friends because of your high commitment to sport? Do they occasionally think you've lost your mind? Jesus' family thought the same of Him.

Mark wrote about a strange incident at chapter 3 and verses 20 and 21, "Then Jesus entered a house, and again a crowd gathered, so that he and his disciples were not even able to eat. When his family heard about this, they went to take charge of him, for they said, 'He is out of his mind.'"

Imagine this, here came Mary and Jesus' brothers and sisters to take him away thinking that he had lost touch with the real world. I know my parents thought I was nuts when I'd skip meals, run miles in sweat clothes and stay after practice every day, just to be a better wrestler.

You are no doubt misunderstood by classmates, friends and even your family when you make sacrifices, prefer teammate relationships to others who don't understand your sport, and when you commit deeply to your team's success over your own convenience or comfort.

That's what winners look like. They commit to their teams and coaches in spite of misunderstanding and questioning. Do like Jesus did and pursue excellence and authentic relationships in today's competition.

ADVERSITY
Micah 7:8

How do you react when you're losing by a wide margin and your opponent rubs salt in your wounds with some trash-talk? How does it feel to lose and to hear the snickers of the winners on their way to the locker room? What should your attitude be in the face of such disrespect?

The prophet Micah had encountered such attitudes and writes about it in chapter 7 and verse 8, "Do not gloat over me, my enemy! Though I have fallen, I will rise. Though I sit in darkness, the Lord will be my light."

Micah advises his triumphant enemy that it would not be wise to gloat over him. He will come back. He also says that though he knew the experience of sitting painfully in the darkness of despair, he would trust the Lord to give him direction for the future.

I love it when a competitor comes back to defeat an earlier trash-talking opponent through perseverance and self-control. I'm impressed by the team that suffers quietly a disappointing loss, only to strengthen their resolve and to compete courageously the next time.

As you prepare for today's competition, guard your heart from the foolish pride that comes with an early lead. Don't gloat over your enemy. Even if you're on the short side of the scoreboard, maintain your attitude and press through to the end, trusting the Lord to be your light to victory.

LEADERSHIP
Mark 4:39-40

Have you ever had a coach or a teammate who could instantly bring peace and order to a chaotic situation? Jesus was that guy for His disciples.

Mark records a remarkable story at chapter 4 and verses 39 through 41, "He got up, rebuked the wind and said to the waves, 'Quiet! Be still!' Then the wind died down and it was completely calm. He said to his disciples, 'Why are you so afraid? Do you still have no faith?'"

In the middle of a furious storm, Jesus was sleeping below the deck of the boat. The panic-stricken disciples woke Him up and thought He didn't care that they were about to die. Jesus calmly dealt with the situation and brought calm from the chaos.

As you compete today, there may be times when chaos and turmoil try to take over your team. There will certainly be some stormy situations that could wreck your team's ship. Who will be the one to restore peace and to speak to the situation?

You can be the person on your team to speak to the chaotic situation in order to restore order. Be the one who says, "Quiet! Be still!" to the situation that's bringing fear to your teammates. Speak confidently and lead your team to a great victory.

INTIMIDATION
Numbers 13:30-33

Who was the most intimidating opponent you ever faced in competition? How did you perceive yourself in comparison with his/her abilities and stature? Did your opponent see you in that same light? Today's scripture tells a similar story.

In the Old Testament book of Numbers at chapter 13 and verses 30 through 33 we read, "Then Caleb silenced the people before Moses and said, 'We should go up and take possession of the land, for we can certainly do it.' But the men who had gone up with him said, 'We can't attack those people; they are stronger than we are.' And they spread among the Israelites a bad report about the land they had explored. They said, 'The land we explored devours those living in it. All the people there are of great size. We saw the Nephilim there. We seemed like grasshoppers in our own eyes, and we looked the same to them.'"

Caleb was about to lose his patience with his teammates. They had seen the greatest place they could ever imagine and he was ready to take possession of the place, but his teammates were all afraid.

Did you hear how they perceived themselves? They said they saw themselves as grasshoppers in comparison to their opponents.

As you compete today, will you see yourselves as Caleb did—fully able to compete with anyone and anywhere? Or will you see yourself as a grasshopper, one totally out of his league?

My challenge to you today is to look your opponent directly in the eye and when you see a reflection of yourself in his eyes, see the image of a champion and not that of a grasshopper.

PRESSURE
Mark 6:30-31

When do you feel the pressures of your life of competition most greatly? Is it on game day, in practice or when surrounded by reporters and fans? Jesus and His followers felt similar pressures and He knew how to handle them.

Let's watch how He deals with the pressing crowd in Mark chapter 6 and verses 30 and 31. "The apostles gathered around Jesus and reported to Him all they had done and taught. Then, because so many people were coming an going that they did not even have a chance to eat, He said to them, 'Come with me by yourselves to a quiet place and get some rest."

Jesus' apostles were coming back from a victorious road trip and they were reporting to Jesus about their successes. They were tired, but excited and had gathered quite a crowd of others who were awed by their accomplishments. Jesus knew just what to do for His most devoted followers.

Rather than hang around with the crowd and its pressures, He calls them away to a more private, quiet place to they could rest. Some of us might be tempted to hang around indefinitely after an important home win, but it might be more prudent to get away with some teammates and close friends for some quiet time of relaxation.

Compete today with great energy and intensity. Pursue excellence in every moment of this contest. But after it's all over, make time to relax, to rest and to unwind with teammates and friends who appreciate you and help take the pressure out of your life. Choose your friends wisely and find peaceful places to relax, far from the foolish and frivolous demands.

COMPASSION
Psalm 103:13-14

Have you ever felt like your coaches or teammates expected more from you than you were capable of giving? How do you handle expectations that seem unreasonable? What do you think God expects of us?

In Psalm 103 and verses 13 and 14, we get an idea of how God tempers His expectations of us. There it reads, "As a father has compassion on his children, so the Lord has compassion on those who fear Him; for He knows how we are formed, He remembers that we are dust."

God knows exactly what we're made of and is thus very compassionate toward us. That's good news. He lovingly cares for us like the best possible father would. Trust Him.

In the world of sport, coaches, teammates, parents, media and others may project expectations that you find unreasonable. If they really care for you, they'll also be compassionate and will know what is truly reasonable. They are the ones you can also trust.

As you prepare to compete today, examine your expectations and those of your teammates and coaching staff. Give your absolute best effort to achieve each one of them. Rest assured that those most committed to you will also be compassionate if their expectations go unmet. They know what you're made of and love you completely.

COURAGEOUS LEADERSHIP
Mark 6:46-51

In your life as a competitor, have you ever experienced great courage and an unnaturally calm spirit in the midst of tremendous struggle and fear? Many of us have and so did Jesus.

We read about such an instance in Mark's gospel at chapter 6 and verses 46 through 51. There it says, "After leaving them, He went up on a mountainside to pray. When evening came, the boat was in the middle of the lake and He was alone on land. He saw the disciples straining at the oars, because the wind was against them. About the fourth watch of the night He went out to them, walking on the lake. He was about to pass by them, but when they saw Him walking on the lake, they thought it was a ghost. They cried out because they all saw Him and were terrified. Immediately He spoke to them and said, 'Take courage! It is I. Don't be afraid.' Then He climbed into the boat with them, and the wind died down."

There are a lot of things happening here, but let's focus on just a few: Great team leaders are aware of the team's condition. Jesus saw that His team was straining at the oars and walked out to check on them.

Great team leaders speak strong words of encouragement to their teammates. Jesus said three simple sentences to His terrified disciples and thus quelled their fears. He said, "Take courage! It is I. Don't be afraid." That was enough.

Great team leaders calm their teammates simply by being present. As soon as Jesus climbed into the boat, the wind died down. Some of you calm things down for your teammates by simply entering the contest. Be such a team leader.

TRUST
Psalm 20:7

On what basis do your opponents or teammates boast? Do they brag about their size and strength? Maybe they talk loudly about their skills, technique or knowledge. Does anyone you know boast in the power of his God?

That's exactly what we hear from David in Psalm 20 and verse 7, "Some trust in chariots and some in horses, but we trust in the name of the Lord our God."

God's power is greater than a whole division of chariots. His strength is mightier than a thousand horses. To David the warrior, God's name is better than all the finest military equipment on the planet.

When your opponent boasts of his speed, God is faster. When your teammate is bragging about his power in the weight room, remember that God is most powerful. When the media boasts of your most recent victories, think about the eternal nature of God's wisdom.

In today's competition, if you must brag at all, make your boast in the one unchanging, immovable person—God almighty.

100%
Mark 12:30

If you were to pick out one principle for competing in your sport as the most important, which would it be? If there were one commandment for life that is primary, what would it be? Jesus spoke clearly about such and His words are recorded in Mark chapter 12 and verse 30.

There we read the most important commandment, "Love the Lord your God with all your heart and will all your soul and with all your mind and with all your strength."

Jesus said that the most important thing in life is to love God like this:

With all your heart—with strong emotional attachment. Love God passionately.

With all your soul—with purposeful, willful desire. Love God on purpose.

With all your mind—with intellectual understanding. Love God wisely.

With all your strength.—with strong physical performance. Love God actively. Love God with 100% of your person, with integrity.

As you prepare today, fix your heart, soul, mind and strength toward competing passionately, purposefully, wisely and actively. That will lead you to a performance that will be pleasing to your teammates, your coaches, the fans and even to God.

DESIRE
Psalm 37:3-4

In what parts of your sport do you find real delight? Which situations or settings give you a wide grin? Maybe it's when you first walk onto the field or court to warm up. Maybe it's the opening minutes of competition. Or maybe it's the look on your opponent's face when he knows you're going to win. Such things are often delightful to people of sport.

King David writes about delightful things in Psalm 37 and verses 3 and 4 where it says, "Trust in the Lord and do good; dwell in the land and enjoy safe pasture. Delight yourself in the Lord and he will give you the desires of your heart."

To this former shepherd, David, to dwell in a land and to enjoy safe pasture would be a great delight. Safety and security would give him a broad smile and a contented heart.

We can experience similarly delightful days when we follow David's instruction. The key seems to be that we trust God and follow his ways. As we place our faith in Him and follow His ways, we will find fulfillment and security in our sport and among our teammates. As we delight ourselves in God's love, we'll see the desires of our hearts come to full fruition.

Compete today in the freedom and security that accompanies those who trust and delight in God.

LOVE YOUR...

Mark 12:31

We talked elsewhere about the most important principle of your sport and about the number one commandment for life. What might be principle and commandment number two?

Jesus voices this second commandment right on the heels of the first in Mark chapter 12 and verse 31, where we read, "The second is this: Love your neighbor as yourself. There is no commandment greater than these."

You've probably heard this for years, but I would like to have you substitute some sport-oriented words for the word "neighbor."

Give this a try...

Love your teammate as yourself. Love your coach as yourself. Love your officials as yourself. Love your opponent as yourself. Love your athletic trainer, equipment manager, even your fans as yourself. That sounds easy, but how do we do this in practical terms?

Do you expect the best of yourself? Expect the same of your teammates. Love them as you do yourself. Do you believe your intentions are pure? Believe the same of others. Love them as you do yourself. Do you desire love and respect? Desire the same for all those around you. Love them as you do yourself.

As you compete in today's contest, extend the love you receive from God to the people who surround you. Whether coach, teammate, fan or official, give each one the love and respect that you desire for yourself.

SACRIFICES
Psalm 51:16-17

What attitudes are most respected and appreciated by your coaches and team leaders? We'd probably list qualities like a strong work ethic, loyalty, teamwork, a willingness to sacrifice and more. What do you suppose would be the attitude most respected by God?

The writer of Psalm 51 answers that question very directly in verses 16 and 17, "You do not delight in sacrifice, or I would bring it; you do not take pleasure in burnt offerings. The sacrifices of God are a broken spirit; a broken and contrite heart, O God, you will not despise."

The writer has found that God's not really impressed with the normal religious sacrifices. Rather, God is very impressed with two primary attitudes. A broken spirit and a contrite heart are of great value to Him.

Those attitudes would serve us well in our pursuit of excellence in sport. A broken spirit is the very opposite of the arrogance so often seen in highly achieving people of sport. A contrite heart is essential to maintaining good teamwork. When one admits his failures or claims the fault for an error to his teammates, he's exhibiting a contrite heart.

As you compete today, maintain a broken spirit and your attitude will win the hearts of your teammates. Compete with a contrite heart and you'll build loyalty and commitment in everyone.

COMPETITIVE INVESTMENTS
Mark 12:41-44

If athletic talent could be measured in dollars and cents, who would be the richest player that you know? How generous is that player in relation to her teammates? Who would be the poorest player that you know? How generous is that person toward others?

Jesus speaks of a similar contrast between rich and poor in Mark chapter 12 and verses 41 through 44. "Jesus sat down opposite the place where the offerings were put and watched the crowd putting their money into the temple treasury. Many rich people threw in large amounts. But a poor widow came and put in two very small copper coins worth only a fraction of a penny. Calling his disciples to him, Jesus said, 'I tell you the truth, this poor widow has put more into the treasury than all the others. They all gave out of their wealth; but she, out of her poverty, put in everything - all she had to live on.'"

Why does it seem that often the poorest of us make the deepest investments in the team? It happens all the time. Often the least talented among us are the best teammates and give to others most generously. It's no surprise; Jesus saw it in His day as well.

Let me challenge you today. Whether athletically rich or poor, invest deeply in your team collectively and in your teammates individually. Give it all away in pursuit of a great team victory.

RENEWED STRENGTH
Psalm 61:1-3

When, in the course of a season, do you begin to lose a little steam? When are you starting to run low on energy? What can you do to regain your strength and vitality?

In Psalm 61 and verse 1 through 3, we hear a poetic prayer for renewed strength. There we read, "Hear my cry, O God; listen to my prayer. From the ends of the earth I call to you, I call as my heart grows faint; lead me to the rock that is higher than I. For you have been my refuge, a strong tower against the foe."

The writer felt totally alienated and exposed. He felt like he was at the edge of the earth and called out to God as his heart grew more and more faint. He saw God as a rock, as a refuge and a strong tower to protect him from his enemies.

You may feel similarly when your strength is waning and all your muscles ache. You may be physically, mentally and emotionally worn out by practice and competition. What are you to do when your hearts grow faint?

As you prepare to compete today, follow the writer's example and cry out to God as a refuge and a strong tower against your foe. Today, that foe may be fatigue or pain. Pray right where you are and He'll be there to support and to protect you.

BETRAYAL
Mark 14:17-19

Have you ever felt betrayed by a coach or a teammate? Maybe something told in confidence was spoken to others or a promise went unfulfilled. Such feelings of betrayal hurt deeply. Imagine if betrayal were to lead to one's death. Such was the case in the life of Jesus.

We read about how Jesus handles a betrayal that hasn't even occurred yet in Mark chapter 14 and verses 17 through 19, "When evening came, Jesus arrived with the Twelve. While they were reclining at the table eating, he said, 'I tell you the truth, one of you will betray me - one who is eating with me.' They were saddened and one by one they said to him, 'Surely not I?'"

Jesus' twelve teammates were all together at something very similar to a pre-game meal when He dropped a bomb on the group. He said that He was aware that one of them would betray Him. It's curious that they would each ask him, "Surely not I?" But it makes sense when we consider that each of them was fully aware that he was certainly capable, given the right circumstances.

These men knew that betrayal is easy, but loyalty is tough. It's easy to betray a confidence, to forward gossip or to turn our backs on our teammates. It's much tougher to be loyal in hard times and to hang in with teammates who perform poorly.

As you prepare for today's competition, be loyal like John. Don't betray your teammates like Judas. Even more, be ready to love extravagantly, like Jesus.

STRENGTH
Psalm 73:26

Take a moment to recall a time when you've competed to the point of total exhaustion. Your body, mind and soul were fully spent in pursuit of a victory. How does one continue to compete, even when at the point of physical breakdown and total collapse? The writer of today's psalm knew what it was for his flesh and his heart to fail.

In Psalm 73 and verse 26 we read, "My flesh and my heart may fail, but God is the strength of my heart and my portion forever."

The writer had lived through times when he had totally exhausted the capacity of his body to fight, but had lived on. He had been to the very end of his heart's ability to love, but found renewed strength of soul.

At the end of your body's natural ability to compete, God is a limitless source of strength. When your heart is poured out like so much water, God is a river of life to your soul.

As you compete today, don't simply rely on the power of your flesh to carry you. Look to God as a continual source of power and strength. Look for His wisdom and joy to carry you through the momentum shifts of the sport. Compete with great strength and passion.

PAIN
Mark 14:35-36

What is there about your life in sport that is so difficult or painful that you wish it would just go away? Maybe it's a nagging injury, the pain of mounting losses or strained relationships with coaches or teammates. Any of these can rip the joy from life.

Jesus faced a similar situation, but the consequences were far greater. We read about it in Mark chapter 14 and verses 35 and 36, "Going a little farther, he fell to the ground and prayed that if possible the hour might pass from him. 'Abba, Father,' he said, 'everything is possible for you. Take this cup from me. Yet not what I will, but what you will.'"

In His last night on the earth, Jesus stared death in the face and knew that He'd be dead in less than 24 hours. As any of us would, He asked that He be spared such pain and suffering. Thankfully, He also had the self-discipline to submit His will to God's.

As you face your every day pains, look for God's will in the matters of life. Don't deny your feelings or hide your displeasure, God knows that it hurts. Talk with Him about it and commit yourself to His purposes in the situation.

In today's competition, take the same attitude toward pain and suffering that Jesus did and press through them to achieve your goals.

Spirit OF A CHAMPION

PRIVILEGE
Psalm 84:10

Have you ever considered how very fortunate you are to participate in sport? There are countless millions of people who would give all they have to be in your positions of privilege.

The writer of Psalm 84 felt such privilege as he wrote the following in verse 10, "Better is one day in your courts than a thousand elsewhere; I would rather be a doorkeeper in the house of my God than dwell in the tents of the wicked."

This person fully realized his great privilege and position. He made very strong comparisons to express it.

If I were to paraphrase his expressions into the language of sport, I might say, "Better is one day on the field of competition than a thousand games watching from the bleachers. I would rather be serving water on the sideline than to watch from the best luxury box in the stadium."

As you prepare to compete today, thank God for the high privilege of being where you are. Rejoice in your position and compete powerfully yet humbly. Be mindful that nearly everyone watching you would give his eye teeth to be where you are. You are truly blessed.

WISDOM
Psalm 90:12

At this point in your sport career, in how many games have you competed? Could you count them? Looking into the future, how many more do you think you have left? That's a sobering question.

Moses, one of the greatest leaders in history, raised a similarly sobering thought in Psalm 90 and verse 12. There it says, "Teach us to number our days aright, that we may gain a heart of wisdom."

Moses could certainly count the days that he had lived in the past, but he also had a grasp of how few he might have left to live. That became the basis for wise living.

Wisdom would have us grasp the significance of each contest. Wisdom would lead us to value every moment we get to spend with our teammates and coaching staff. If our hearts are full of wisdom, we will be aware of the brevity of our careers in sport and will drain every drop of good from them.

As you prepare for competition, take some time to pray and to thank God for all the days of your past. Ask Him to fill your heart with wisdom as you seek to grasp the significance of each moment, every practice and today's contest.

TRUST
Psalm 56:3-4

What situations in your sport tend to produce fear in you or your teammates? How do you deal with fear when it appears? Who can we trust when we're assaulted by fear and anxiety?

David, the psalmist, wrote the following words in Psalm 56 and verses 3 and 4, "When I am afraid, I will trust in you. In God, whose word I praise, in God I trust; I will not be afraid. What can mortal man do to me?"

You'll notice that he didn't say that he was never afraid. Rather, he said that when he was afraid, he would trust in God. He trusted in one who is far greater than any mortal man.

There are plenty of moments in sport that produce fear. We may find ourselves afraid of injury. Many of us compete, nagged by a constant fear of failure. Others may even fear their opponents.

In any case, when we are afraid, let's put our trust in God. He's with us every moment and is able to dispel every fear and doubt from our minds.

As you pray in preparation for this day's competition, commit yourself to God's care. Trust Him with every detail of your sport. In His care you're safe, what can mortal man do to you?

DREAMS FULFILLED
Psalm 126:1-3

Take a moment to recall a time when your sport dreams were realized. Perhaps it was a championship won, a rival beaten or an individual award achieved. The Bible shares a poetic look at dreams fulfilled in today's scripture.

Psalm 126 and verses 1 through 3 reads, "When the Lord brought back the captives to Zion, we were like men who dreamed. Our mouths were filled with laughter, our tongues with songs of joy. Then it was said among the nations, The Lord has done great things for them. The Lord has done great things for us, and we are filled with joy."

The writer remembered returning home after a long absence. It was almost too good to believe, like a dream. He remembered the laughter and the joyful singing of his friends and family. The people from surrounding countries were amazed. Even more, he remembered the source of these blessings.

It's so much fun for us to see our dreams fulfilled and our goals achieved. Our mouths are filled with laughter and we exult in every victory. Those who watch you compete even join in the fun. Occasionally we'll even remember to thank the ultimate source of all that's good... God.

During today's competition, give your best effort to see your dreams fulfilled and your goals achieved. Don't be surprised when people comment like they did in the psalm, "The Lord has done great things for them." You can echo their comment in grateful prayer with a wide grin on your face.

PRACTICE
Psalm 126:5-6

What part of practice and conditioning seems to be just plain old hard work? Has such a workout ever pushed you to the point of total exhaustion and even tears? Today's scripture relates exactly to that level of physical and emotional expense.

In Psalm 126 and verses 5 and 6 we read, "Those who sow in tears will reap with songs of joy. He who goes out weeping, carrying seed to sow, will return with songs of joy, carrying sheaves with him."

These people knew the pain and hardship of working on a farm in the early spring. Lots of hours and draining labor. They also knew the joy and exhilaration of a great harvest in the fall.

You know the value of grueling practice sessions and punishing workouts. They produce a fruitful and even fun reward at season's end. Those brutal preseason days of conditioning pay off in the postseason with exciting victories.

Invest yourself in tough, intense practices and you'll reap a harvest of game days filled with joyous wins. Compete today with confidence knowing that you've made the investments that will pay off in today's contest.

HUMILITY
Psalm 131:1

How do you react when teammates or fans criticize your coaches' decisions? Sometimes you might nod in agreement or even voice your displeasure. At other times you might simply remain silent or vigorously defend the staff's strategy. What attitudes might be revealed by those various reactions?

In Psalm number 131 and verse 1 we read David's view on important attitudes. There we read, "My heart is not proud, O Lord, my eyes are not haughty; I do not concern myself with great matters or things too wonderful for me." Here's one of history's great leaders and he said that he had to guard his attitude from arrogant pride.

We've all seen haughty eyes that look down on everyone else. The arrogant heart has an opinion on everything and is fully convinced of his superiority.

Let's guard our attitudes and put on humility like David. Let's not be so proud or foolish to suppose that our few years of competition make us wiser than our coaches whose decades of experience far surpass our own. Let's not concern ourselves with the great matters of the sport nor with things beyond our ability to understand.

In today's competition, be the competitor you were made to be. Do so with great humility and relax under the leadership of your wise, talented coaching staff.

TEAM UNITY
Psalm 133:1

How would you describe the sense of team unity experienced by this team? What are the benefits that accompany a team with great unity versus a team that is full of strife, contention and selfish attitudes?

Today's scripture describes such unity in Psalm 133 and verse 1. There we read, "How good and pleasant it is when brothers live together in unity!" Simple, huh? The psalmist says that unity produces an atmosphere that is good and pleasant. It's simple to describe, but harder to produce.

Team unity is good, leading to the best possible performance from everyone related to the team. Unity brings out the best in each player, coach, trainer, equipment manager, etc...

Team unity is pleasant, smoothing out every potential conflict and contention. Every team is made up of vastly different people. It's supposed to be that way. Team unity allows us to maintain a focus on our common goals, aspirations and values. That makes the living together pleasant.

In today's competition, let great team unity produce an atmosphere of goodness and pleasance. Strive together to see each teammate compete to his highest capacity. Keep your focus on unifying words and actions that make the whole process pleasant for everyone concerned. Compete in unified way and you'll be unstoppable.

THOUGHTS
Psalm 139:17-18

How much thoughtful preparation goes into a single competition for you? If we were to total up the collective hours of thought, contemplation, analysis, dreaming, visualization and anticipation among your teammates and coaching staff, the sum would be staggering. How much do you believe God thinks about you? How often are you at the front of his mind? Who could calculate such a number?

We get a glimpse at how God thinks in Psalm 139 and verses 17 and 18. Here's how David described these ideas, "How precious concerning me are your thoughts, O God! How vast is the sum of them! Were I to count them, they would outnumber the grains of sand. When I awake, I am still with you."

David was overwhelmed with the concept that an all-powerful God would spend His time thinking of him. That's a little staggering for me too! He has a universe to run, but He's concerned with every detail of my life.

The largest number David can conceive of is the number of grains of sand on the earth, but that's a smaller number than the sum of God's thoughts concerning each one of us.

For me, that leads to a great deal of confidence. I draw great comfort from knowing that my life is not hidden in a corner out of God's view. Rather He's intimately aware of every facet of my life and my every concern.

Let these words from the Psalms result in a great confidence and assurance that every moment of this day is in the center of God's attention for each one of us. His thoughts toward us are precious, innumerable and always loving.

REAL POWER
Psalm 147:10-11

In which part of your sport do you have the greatest sense of strength or power? Maybe it's in the weight room, maybe during drills in practice, or even on game day when it's all on the line. How central is that feeling to your enjoyment of the sport?

In Psalm 147 and verses 10 and 11 we read about where God senses power and strength. It reads, "His pleasure is not in the strength of the horse, nor His delight in the legs of a man; the Lord delights in those who fear Him, who put their hope in His unfailing love."

It seems that God is impressed with neither the normal measurements of strength nor the usual vessels for power. Neither the strongest horse nor the fittest athlete really brings him pleasure. Rather He is deeply pleased by those who respect and trust Him.

Most coaches are like this too. They might seem impressed at first with the very talented player, the powerful athlete with strength and speed, but if you hang around with them you'll hear stories about their real favorites. They are the ones who "bought in" and trusted their coaches. They are the ones who built unity among their teammates and gave themselves up to make the team better.

Good coaches, like the Lord Himself, find pleasure and take delight in the players who show respect and display trust. Make that your aim in today's competition and you'll be exhibiting real power and strength.

PRIVILEGE
Psalm 16:5-6

How much are you a student of your sport? Do you know its history and traditions? Who are the key figures in your own program's history? The Bible is full of stories and even poetry that recount the history of God's people.

In the Hebrew book of Poetry called Psalms at chapter 16 and verses 5 and 6 we read, "Lord, you have assigned me my portion and my cup; you have made my lot secure. The boundary lines have fallen for me in pleasant places; surely I have a delightful inheritance."

The writer was well aware of his blessed heritage. He credited God with putting him in position to be even further blessed. He described his place in life as secure, pleasant and delightful.

As you are in preparation for today's competition, let your mind page back through the players and coaches from this program's past. Remember their names and the heritage in which you now live. Recall the achievements of those who have gone before you. You'll probably join the psalm writer in seeing your position as secure, pleasant and even delightful.

Spirit OF A CHAMPION

SACRIFICES
Psalm 51:16-17

What attitudes are most respected and appreciated by your coaches and team leaders? We'd probably list qualities like a strong work ethic, loyalty, teamwork, a willingness to sacrifice and more. What do you suppose would be the attitude most respected by God?

The writer of Psalm 51 answers that question very directly in verses 16 and 17, "You do not delight in sacrifice, or I would bring it; you do not take pleasure in burnt offerings. The sacrifices of God are a broken spirit; a broken and contrite heart, O God, you will not despise."

The writer has found that God's not really impressed with the normal religious sacrifices. Rather, God is very impressed with two primary attitudes. A broken spirit and a contrite heart are of great value to Him.

Those attitudes would serve us well in our pursuit of excellence in sport. A broken spirit is the very opposite of the arrogance so often seen in highly achieving people of sport. A contrite heart is essential to maintaining good teamwork. When one admits his failures or claims the fault for an error to his teammates, he's exhibiting a contrite heart.

As you compete today, maintain a broken spirit and your attitude will win the hearts of your teammates. Compete with a contrite heart and you'll build loyalty and commitment in everyone.